DANDE

puffs

MW01689592

Illustrated by Lynne Tracey

Mistress Pratt

Mistress Pratt,
Round and fat,
By accident sat
Upon her hat.

She squashed it flat —
And that was that!

Arnold Lobel

Miss Mary Mac

Miss Mary **Mac, Mac, Mac,**
All dressed in **black, black, black,**
With silver **buttons, buttons, buttons,**
All down her **back, back, back.**

She asked her **mother, mother, mother,**
For fifteen **cents, cents, cents,**
To see the **elephant, elephant, elephant,**
Jump over the **fence, fence, fence.**

He jumped so **high, high, high,**
Till he reached the **sky, sky, sky,**
And didn't come **back, back, back,**
Till the Fourth of **July, ly, ly.**

Traditional

Meg's Egg

Meg
Likes
A *reg*ular egg

Not a poached
Or a fried
But a *reg*ular egg

Not a deviled
Or coddled
Or scrambled
Or boiled

But an *egg*ular
*Meg*ular
*Reg*ular
Egg!

Mary Ann Hoberman

What Is Red?

Red is a sunset
Blazy and bright.

Red is feeling brave
With all your might.

Red is a sunburn
Spot on your nose.

Sometimes red
Is a red, red rose.

Mary O'Neill

Mr. Rabbit

Mr. Rabbit has a habit
That is very cute to see.

He wrinkles up and crinkles up
His little nose at me.

I like my little rabbit,
And I like his little brother,

And we have a lot of fun
Making faces at each other!

D. Wilson

Our Washing Machine

Our washing machine went whisity whirr,
Whisity, whisity, whirr.

One day at noon it went whisity *click*!
Whisity, whisity, whisity, *click*!
Click, ***grr***, *click*, ***grr***, *click*, ***grr***, *click*!

Call the repairman.
Fix it . . . Quick!

Patricia Hubbell

A Rocket in My Pocket

I've got a rocket
In my pocket;
I cannot stop to play.
Away it goes!
I've burned my toes.
It's Independence Day.

Cock a Doodle Doo

Cock a doodle doo!
My dame has lost her shoe,
My master's lost his fiddling stick
And knows not what to do.

Cock a doodle doo!
What is my dame to do?
Till master finds his fiddling stick,
She'll dance without her shoe.

Cock a doodle doo!
My dame has found her shoe.
And master's found his fiddling stick,
Sing *doodle doodle doo*.

Traditional

Lumps

Humps are lumps
and so are mumps.

Bumps make lumps
on heads.

Mushrooms grow
in clumps of lumps —
on clumps of stumps,
in woods and dumps.

Springs spring lumps
in beds.

Mosquito bites
make itchy lumps.

Frogs on logs
make twitchy lumps.

Judith Thurman

Jumpy Grumpy Mouse

A jumpy, grumpy mouse
Lives in a dumpy house
All made of dandelion
puffs
puffs
puffs
You are welcome to his cheese,
But please don't sneeze,
Or good-bye to the grumpy mouse,
Good-bye to the dumpy house,
Good-bye to the dandelion
puffs
puffs
puffs
Good-bye to
the dandelion puffs.

Ellen Raskin

Hiccup Cure

Want to cure your hiccups quick?
Stick out your tongue and bite your lip.
Hold your breath and shake one hip.
Pull back your left foot and kick up.
Now, you see, we've cured your hiccup.
Nothing much to it —
Don't you feel swell?

Shel Silverstein

Two Ducks

I saw two ducks with chicken pox.
A most amusing paradox.
But one thing I have never seen
Is a whooping crane eat a coffee bean.

Ellen Raskin

Dance to Your Daddy

Dance to your daddy,
My little babby,
Dance to your daddy,
My little lamb.

You shall have a fishy
In a little dishy,
You shall have a fishy
When the boat comes in.

You shall have an apple,
You shall have a plum,
You shall have a rattle-basket
When your daddy comes home.

Traditional

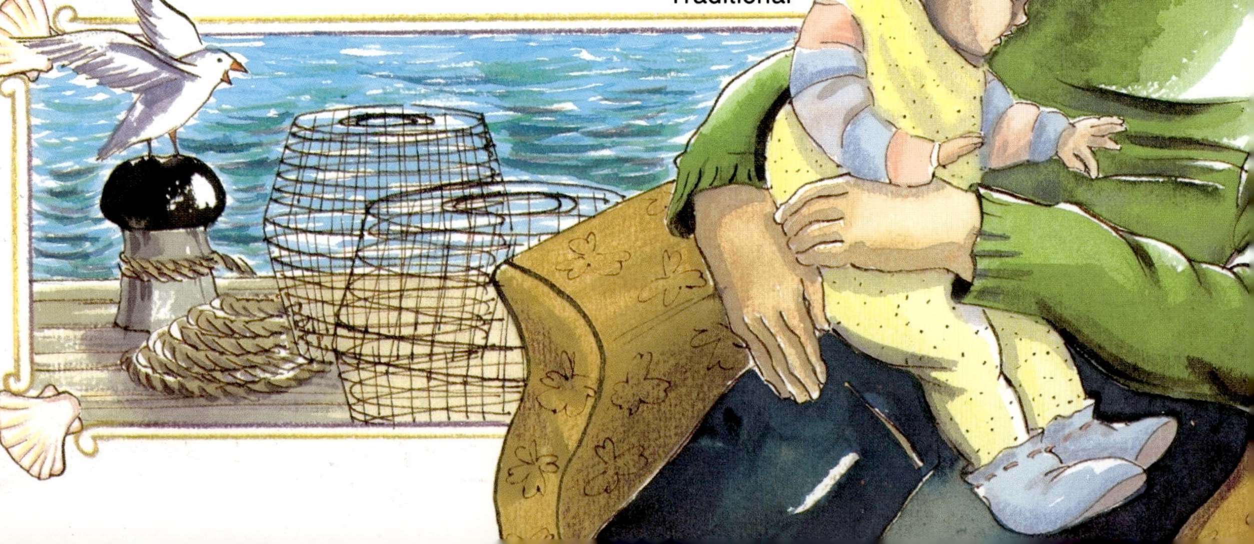

Hickety Pickety

Hickety, pickety, my black hen,
She lays eggs for gentlemen.
Gentlemen come every day
To see what my black hen doth lay.

Traditional

A Long-Haired Griggle

A long-haired Griggle
from the land of Grunch,
Always giggled
when he ate his lunch.
He'd wiggle and giggle,
and munch and crunch
While nibbling the pebbles
that he liked for lunch.

Alice Gilbert

Song of the Train

Clickety-clack,
Wheels on the track,
This is the way
They begin the attack.
Click-ety-clack,
Click-ety-clack,
Click-ety-clack-ety,
Click-ety
Clack.

Clickety-clack

Over the crack,
Faster and faster
The song of the track.

Clickety-clack,
Clickety-clack,
Clickety-clackety,
Clickety
Clack.

Riding in front,
Riding in back,
Everyone hears
The song of the track.

Clickety-clack,
Clickety-clack,
Clickety-clackety,
Clickety
Clack.

David McCord

Baloney Belly Billy

Baloney Belly Billy
swallows anything for cash,
if you offer him a penny,
he'll chew paper from the trash,
he'll eat guppies for a nickel,
for a dime, he'll eat a bug,
and a quarter will convince him
that he ought to eat a slug.

I have seen him eat a button,
I have seen him eat a bee,
I have seen him eat three beetles
for a half a dollar fee,
for a dollar he will gladly
eat a lizard off a fence,
just imagine what he'd swallow
for another fifty cents.

Jack Prelutsky

Nobody

Nobody loves me,
Nobody cares,
Nobody picks me nectarines and pears.

Nobody offers me eggnog and Cokes,
Nobody notices and laughs at my jokes.

Nobody helps when I get in a fight,
Nobody does all my homework at night.

Nobody misses me,
Nobody cries,
Nobody thinks I'm a really nice guy.

Shel Silverstein

V Is for the Vendor

V is for the vendor,
  A very vocal man.
He drives about in summer
  In a vegetable van.

And everybody listens
  To his voice upon the breeze,
Calling, "Strawberries, strawberries!
  Fresh green peas!"

Phyllis McGinley

I Am Running in a Circle

I am running in a circle
and my feet are getting sore,
and my head is spinning
spinning
as it's never spun before,
I am dizzy
dizzy
dizzy.
Oh! I cannot bear much more,
I am trapped in a revolving
. . . volving
. . . volving
. . . volving door!

Jack Prelutsky

Zapper Zockke

The machine began to sizzle
as the points began to mount,
he zapped so many space sardines
that even *he* lost count.

Then, in a flash, he vanished,
for he moved at such a pace,
that he spun into a time warp —
Zapper Zockke's in hyperspace! Jack Prelutsky

Alphabet

A my name is Anna.
My husband's name is Albert.
I come from Alaska.
And we sell Apples.

B my name is Betty.
My husband's name is Bob.
I come from Boston.
And we sell Bottles.

C my name is Clarisa.
My husband's name is Charley.
I come from Columbus.
And we sell Cats.

Unknown